Successful Telephone Selling

If you want to know how...

Organising a Conference
How to plan and run a successful event

Successful Negotiating
Getting what you want in the best possible way

Understanding Small Business Accounting
*Learn the essentials of financial accounting and
stay in control of your business*

The Ultimate Business plan
Essential planning skills to get you where you want to be

Make Meetings Work

howtobooks

Please send for a free copy of the latest catalogue:

How To Books
3 Newtec Place, Magdalen Road
Oxford OX4 1RE, United Kingdom
email: info@howtobooks.co.uk
http://www.howtobooks.co.uk

Successful
Telephone
Selling

Richard Hession

howtobooks

Published by How To Books Ltd,
3 Newtec Place, Magdalen Road,
Oxford OX4 1RE. United Kingdom.
Tel: (01865) 793806. Fax: (01865) 248780
email: info@howtobooks.co.uk
http://www.howtobooks.co.uk

British Library Cataloguing in Publication Data.
A catalogue record for this book is available from the British Library.

Cover design by Baseline Arts Ltd, Oxford
Produced for How To Books by Deer Park Productions, Tavistock
Typeset by PDQ Typesetting, Newcastle-under-Lyme, Staffordshire
Printed and bound in Great Britain by Cromwell Press, Trowbridge,
Wiltshire.

NOTE: The material contained in this book is set out in good faith
for general guidance and no liability can be accepted for loss or
expense incurred as a result of relying in particular circumstances on
statements made in this book. Laws and regulations are complex and
liable to change, and readers should check the current position with
the relevant authorities before making personal arrangements.

Contents

Preface

Grateful thanks must go to all those who have
exerted influences in my life as a sales manager –
too numerous to mention here. They run from my
various mentors in the companies for which I have
been fortunate to work, through to the professional
trainers and coaches who have made such a
positive impact to improving my sales focus and
results. Particular thanks to Frederick J. Nixon for
his invaluable assistance in the editing of this
book.

Remember:

Winners never quit and quitters never win!

Richard Hession

Bear these positive qualities in mind when you pick up a telephone – AND SMILE!

adaptable/alert/articulate/assertive/awake/bright/
calm/caring/concerned/concise/confident/
consistent/controlled/diplomatic/efficient/flexible/
friendly/helpful/humorous/informed/intelligent/
keen/knowledgeable/patient/persuasive/pleasant/
polite/positive/practical/prepared/professional/
proficient/purposeful/relaxed/reliable/respectful/
responsible/sensible/sincere/sympathetic/tactful/
tolerant/understanding

With all telephone calls remember KISS (Keep It Short and Sweet). And when you have struck gold, stop digging!

Banish any
negatives like
these from your mind
– A FROWN DRAGS
YOU DOWN!

abrupt/aggressive/angry/argumentative/arrogant/
biased/bored/casual/chewing/critical/deceitful/
demanding/distracted/grovelling/hesitant/ignorant/
impatient/indecisive/irritable/loud/miserable/
munching/negative/obsequious/patronising/
pompous/prejudiced/rude/sarcastic/smoking/
superior/swearing/threatening/timid/uncertain/
untruthful/vague/whispering

Dial a
smile!

Chapter 1

Handling Incoming Calls

In this Chapter:

- **correct use of the phone**
- **telephone courtesy**
- **'on-hold' rules**
- **transferring calls**
- **taking messages**
- **questioning techniques.**

For many existing or potential customers their first and regular contact is by telephone. First-time callers will start forming an impression of your company from the moment you answer the telephone. The way in which you handle their call gives them a ready indication of the level of service they can expect.

First impressions really do count when it comes to how you handle incoming calls, whether you are an operator on the switchboard of a large organisation or answering the telephone in your department. Although unable to speak with you face to face, a caller will nevertheless build up an impression of you and your company from the tone of your voice, what you say and how you say it. Projecting your voice over the phone is a technique acquired with practice and experience. A telephone enhances well modulated tones, but exaggerates any peculiarities in the voice of the person treating it like a megaphone. There is no need to bellow.

> *Be yourself, be natural and don't put on a 'telephone voice'. An accent or dialect is not something of which to be ashamed. Don't try to disguise it. It helps establish your personality.*

Insincerity, sarcasm or disinterest easily comes across on the telephone. It is vital to appear interested, professional and enthusiastic at all times. You never know if someone is phoning your company just to make comparisons with others in the same field.

Is this you?

❓ *Not the phone again! Well, I don't care who it is, they can wait – I'm busy!*

❓ *Let it ring. If it's important they'll ring again.*

❓ *Hello – who? Hold on a jiff while I get a bit of paper.*

❓ *Oh, still there? I'll try to put you through.*

❓ *She's not in. Try ringing this afternoon.*

❓ *Yeah, dunno when that'll be, but I'll see what we can do – OK? Cheers.*

Correct use of the phone

In this age of ever-developing IT wizardry, the telephone still remains one of the best forms of communication, second only to speaking with someone directly face to face. Like every good tool or instrument the telephone, when used correctly, is an excellent aid. But it is not just a question of picking up the receiver and speaking. You have to acquire the right technique.

To begin with there are some basic rules:

- Before answering the phone, prepare yourself mentally and concentrate on what you are going to say.

- Always answer the phone promptly and don't let it ring more than twice, even if you are dealing with other things.

- Sit upright and lift the receiver to your ear; don't bend down to take your ear to the phone.

- Pause, breathe, speak – smile!

- Speak slowly, clearly, and sound friendly and welcoming: and smile again!

Telephone courtesy

Bad telephone manners result from lack of consideration for the person at the other end. There's a temptation to take advantage of the lack of personal contact, and shelter behind the partial anonymity that the telephone affords. We all know people who, aware that the caller cannot see them, are guilty of gesticulating, grimacing or yawning to amuse their office colleagues.

Many a good sale has been lost because a potential customer has been irritated by the lack of courtesy shown to them over the telephone. There is an etiquette everyone should observe when using the telephone. Quite simply it's this: show the same courtesy to telephone callers as you would if you were dealing with them face to face.

As a start:

◆ Never just answer 'Hello'. Begin with 'good morning/afternoon'.

◆ Identify yourself by stating your name and department.

◆ Follow up with 'May I help you?'

◆ If it's necessary to screen calls, a polite 'May I ask who's calling?' is the way to do it, not just a blunt 'Who's calling?'

◆ Explain and apologise for any delays in transferring calls.

◆ Do not leave your caller wondering what's happening – report back every 50 to 60 seconds.

◆ Show your willingness to take a message.

- End the call with a polite 'Thank you' or 'You're welcome' and 'Goodbye'.

'On-hold' rules

When putting a caller on hold to make enquiries on their behalf, follow this sequence of action:

- **Why** → explain why it's necessary to keep them on hold, selling them the benefits of your company's products or services.

- **Where** → decide which person or department will be able to sort out the query.

- **How long** → give the caller an estimate of the expected timescale of the delay before you can answer their query.

- **What** → assess the information you have obtained and pass on the good news to the caller.

- **Offer** → the caller an alternative if the timescale is unacceptable or inconvenient to them.

> *Avoid too many ring-back alternatives. The best policy is to clear problems at the first opportunity.*

◆ **Ask** → the caller if any further information is required to avoid further on-hold situations during the same call.

Transferring calls

There are two things that drive customers to distraction. The first is not being able to get through to a number, particularly if it just rings and rings without anybody answering. The second is being left hanging on the line while a call is being transferred to someone else. Following these rules will ensure the smooth and efficient transfer of calls:

◆ **Why** → explain to the caller why a transfer is necessary.

◆ **Determine** → the caller's precise requirements to ensure you transfer them correctly.

◆ **Who and where** → tell the caller to whom they are being transferred, giving name, title, department, and extension number.

- ◆ **Ask** → the caller's telephone number and name, just in case the call is cut off.

- ◆ **Hold** → explain to the caller why you might have to put them on hold, for example, locating a contact in a large office.

- ◆ **Explain** → give the new contact to whom the caller is to be transferred all the relevant facts as you know them.

If the new contact is not available or is engaged, you have to decide:

(a) whether to try an alternative contact
(b) ask the caller to ring back later, or
(c) take a message.

Message taking

Always be prepared to write down the details – it guarantees accuracy and avoids unnecessary callbacks to find out further information that you should have obtained from the start. Always keep paper and pen or pencil by the telephone. You'll need to record the date, time, caller's name and telephone number, together with any message. Also include your own name.

Printed pads which make copies are available from office stationers. They are preferable to loose bits of paper, which tend to get buried or lost altogether.

Questioning techniques

Develop a good questioning technique. It shows you are interested in helping the customer and can save a great deal of time and frustration for everyone – the caller, you as the person answering the telephone and any of your colleagues likely to become involved. Here's an example:

Operator: 'Good afternoon, how can I help you?'

Caller: 'I want to speak to the manager.'

Operator: 'One moment, please. I'll see if she's available. May I say who's calling?' (rings extension) 'Miss Green? A call for you.' (Back to caller) I'm putting you through.'

Manager: 'Good afternoon.'

Caller:	'Could you give me some idea when my delivery will be arriving on Friday, so that I can prepare the people in my stores?'
Manager:	'I'm sorry, I don't have those details to hand. I'll just put you through to our transport department – they'll be able to help you.'

One simple question from the operator – 'May I ask what it's about?' – would have saved everyone a lot of time. The caller could have been put through to the transport department without delay. Knowing the reason for a customer's call allows you to:

◆ deal with the call yourself or transfer it to the correct department

◆ pass on the details to the eventual recipient of the call, so that they have time to think (particularly useful if the caller is aggrieved).

We should ask questions to:

◆ gain information and pass it on accurately

◆ establish the details of a customer's needs

- discover any underlying problems, queries, fears and buying objections

- develop relationships and put the customer at ease

- show interest in the customer and their business

- make them feel justifiably important

- help define the correct route to sorting out problems and queries

- maintain and enhance our own company's image.

Questions used correctly and logically:

- build confidence and improve sales results

- save time and money and reduce mistakes

- keep control of the call

- maintain the customer's cool.

In summary...

- **Develop good telephone manners. Treat the**

caller with the same courtesy as you would if
you were speaking face to face.

◆ Smile and be yourself – it's the basis for creating
a good telephone manner and puts the caller at
their ease.

◆ Make your greeting clear and friendly. Speak
slowly and distinctly, so that the caller knows
your name and that of your company.

◆ Transfer calls quickly and efficiently to the right
person. Avoid frustration and ill feeling which
results from unnecessary delays.

◆ Record messages accurately and make sure they
are going to be dealt with promptly.

◆ Use your questioning technique skills to find out
what the caller requires, and show that you are
interested in helping them.

Chapter 2

Problem Calls

In this Chapter:
- **preparing yourself**
- **listening carefully**
- **establishing a rapport**
- **confirming a course of action**
- **following through.**

Look upon difficult phone calls as a challenge. If they're complaints treat them as sales opportunities. As well as retaining customers and keeping them happy, aim to increase existing orders. You are, after all, in the sales game.

Like a driver behind the wheel of a car, people on the telephone often undergo a complete personality change. Normally well-balanced individuals become more angry, rude and aggressive than they would be if they were complaining to you face to face. You are a voice, an anonymous person they can vent their frustrations on and really let rip. They're likely to become more and more worked up as the minutes tick by, particularly if they are trying to impress their manager who is listening in to the conversation.

One thing is certain, if you have not already experienced them, you're going to get plenty of difficult telephone calls during your telesales career, so be positive and turn them to your advantage. When dealing with complaints and queries listen carefully, make notes and, above all, keep your cool and maintain that smile. Be sympathetic and diplomatic. Let the caller let off steam (it's your job to listen). Don't look upon difficult calls as a nuisance. After all, if customers aren't able to make you aware of their dissatisfaction, they'll stop dealing with you and tell others your company is no good. When people take the trouble to complain, it means that they do at least care, and have the potential of being loyal and long term customers if handled correctly.

The quicker you settle a complaint and provide the right encouragement, the more likely you are to secure a customer's loyalty.

You are a professional. You have a highly developed thick skin. Just deal with it – it is *not* personal!

Is this you?

❓ *Any complaint is a pain in the neck as far as I'm concerned.*

❓ *Do I have to speak to them on the phone? Why can't they write in?*

❓ *No, I don't need to take down the details. It's probably the usual moan about late delivery.*

❓ *I've had a bad enough day already. If they start going on, I'll tell them what I think and see how they deal with that!*

❓ *Who can we pass the buck to?*

❓ *I'll fob them off with the old excuse about shortage of staff or the system going down.*

❓ *They're not what you might call good customers of ours anyway.*

Preparing yourself

When you are about to handle a telephone call you suspect is likely to be a difficult one, bear the

Scout motto in mind and 'Be prepared'. Adopt a positive attitude – have confidence in your own ability to resolve any problems or queries to the caller's satisfaction and your own. Above all, don't panic and don't take things personally.

> *By being professional and objective in your approach, you will avoid getting emotionally involved or upset by taking the complaint personally.*

Smile and go with the flow. Chill out – deal with it and let it wash over you. This is what funds your lifestyle.

Problems are challenges that enable us to exercise our ingenuity and increase our experience. Rid your mind of negative thoughts. You are going to turn what lesser mortals might see as a setback into a successful outcome for you and your firm – a result!

Having prepared yourself mentally, take these steps to complete your state of readiness:

◆ Get the call transferred, if necessary, to an extension where it's quiet and you won't be overheard by other clients or customers.

♦ Have paper and pen ready to take notes. Noting down details will help you to keep calm and collected.

♦ Make sure you have any necessary files or paperwork readily at hand to refer to. In the case of every complaint or query, establishing the facts is all important.

Listening carefully

Let complaining customers have their say. Listen intently and don't interrupt until they've finished. They won't want to hear anything you have to say until they've got the problem off their chest. Encourage them to give you the whole story. Make notes of the complaint or query, including their name and telephone number, right at the start in case you are cut off. Ask any relevant questions to establish all the facts.

> *Check with the caller to ensure you have everything correctly recorded. That way there cannot be any misunderstanding.*

Encourage information to assist in finding a solution. Show some understanding with such phrases as:

◆ 'Yes, I can understand why you are annoyed.'

◆ 'I see, I'm with you.'

◆ 'Then what happened?'

◆ 'Please go on, tell me more.'

It's preferable to offer to ring back if you need to investigate further. If you do have to leave the customer holding on, explain why:

◆ 'If you could hold on for just a moment, Mr . . . I will look up your order.'

◆ 'Sorry about the delay, Mr . . . If you could bear with us for a few minutes we'll check and get back to you. Is that acceptable?'

Analysis shows that a business is likely to lose most of its customers – 68% – because of indifference on the part of its sales and service personnel. Of the others, 1% die, 3% move, 5% develop other relationships, 9% move for price and 14% for quality reasons, i.e. two-thirds could be down to you!

Establishing a rapport

To discuss any problem rationally, you need to build a bond between you and the complainant. Apologise if you or your company is undoubtedly in the wrong, but don't abjectly grovel to win an irate customer over – you'll lose their respect.

> *Don't plead for sympathy. That's as bad as an abject apology. As a representative of your firm you must be prepared to take the flak as well as share the praise.*

Don't demoralise yourself into hating your job.

There are other ways of getting them to feel that you're on their side and trying to do your best to sort things out. Without establishing this rapport, you won't get anywhere in your endeavours to bring them round to your way of thinking. So after the initial stages of your conversation:

◆ Start building a bridge to discuss the problem sensibly and dispassionately.

◆ In addition to getting the bare facts, ask questions to gain further clarification.

◆ Read them your notes to help them and you get things in perspective and clear in both your minds.

◆ Use their name whenever possible. Everyone likes to hear their own name.

◆ Impress on them that your desire is to reach a satisfactory solution.

◆ Deal with the problem in a thoroughly sympathetic and professional manner.

◆ Don't argue, it will only make matters worse, as will losing your temper.

◆ Don't look for a fall guy to put the blame on. Never attempt to pretend it's nothing to do with you.

Confirming a course of action

Only a sales person knows the great buzz felt when winning back a customer. You're the one who has to come up with a solution to the complaint, but you'll find it readily in the product or service itself you're selling. Correctly handled, complaints and other difficult calls can be turned to your advantage.

> *As well as retaining customer confidence, you could be increasing sales – and earnings!*

Let's recap. So far you've:

◆ listened and made notes

◆ acknowledged the customer's complaint with caring and understanding

◆ apologised if necessary

◆ asked questions to rebuild confidence and maintain a good relationship between the customer and your company.

Now it's time to plan sensible action – and to go on selling for the future. Make the customer your partner in determining the course of action. Consult them and ask them what they think should happen. You will be amazed by their answers. Something along the lines of, 'I'm sure you've already given the situation a lot of thought. I'm not quite clear myself how to solve the problem, but I'm sure you have some good ideas', will prompt a positive response. Often they just want to talk to you about their frustration.

> *Having got it off their chest they will feel much better. It could be that they just want a straightforward apology.*

Choose your words carefully. Instead of saying, 'I can't get it to you until Monday', tell the customer, 'No problem. I'll be glad to send it out to you for Monday.' Having discussed a course of action that meets with approval from the customer, confirm it by:

◆ Checking that all details are clear and understandable to prevent possible future misunderstandings.

◆ Go through the course of action step by step in logical sequence with the customer and get their agreement at every stage.

◆ Reinforce the feeling of 'partnership' with 'Let's be sure we're both clear about what we will do next', rather than 'I want to be sure you understand what I intend doing.'

◆ Conclude your call by seeking an assurance from the customer that you are both in agreement on everything.

Carrying out a thorough complaints handling procedure is vital. If you automatically side with the customer right from the word go, it could suggest to them that problems happen all too often!

Following through

A course of action agreed between you and the customer will be so many wasted words unless you make sure it is followed through with attention to detail. Before signing off, make sure the customer is no longer angry and that their faith is restored in you and your company. Assure them that matters will be put right, but don't just leave it there.

To make doubly sure they will not be among the 68% of customers lost through indifference on the part of sales and service personnel, it's well worth:

◆ Thanking them for having taken the trouble to bring the problem to your attention and giving you a chance to put it right.

◆ Saying you're sorry they've been upset.

♦ Assuring them the last thing your company
   wants to do is upset its customers.

As soon as possible after you come off the
telephone, get things moving. Make sure that the
action you are taking is strictly along the lines
agreed with the customer. Plan and co-ordinate
each step carefully. If you need to involve others
in your company, impress upon them the
importance of them playing their part in helping
to put things right to the customer's satisfaction.

> *There's nothing worse than finding out all too late
> that nothing has been done and the customer is
> on the telephone more irate than ever.*

So choose the key people who will be involved and
use positive words when you talk to them to
reinforce the need for successful action. And check
and recheck at every stage that things are
happening. When you next contact the customer
regarding doing further business, set aside any
thoughts of what has gone wrong in the past.
Remember instead what you did to put things
right.

In summary...

◆ Be a good listener and define the real difficulty or the exact objection being raised right from the start. Allow the caller to let off steam without interrupting or taking personal offence.

◆ Pause after they have finished, to show consideration. Appreciate genuine frustration and anger. Make it obvious to the customer that you understand and care.

◆ Be sorry for the upset caused without apologising for apparently doing wrong. Until the true facts are known, it might not necessarily be your company's fault.

◆ Involve the caller in reaching a solution. Reduce tension, endeavour to maintain your relationship, and rebuild customer confidence. Stress your commitment to sensible and effective action.

◆ Plan the action step by step and see that it is carried out, checking that details are as agreed with the customer.

◆ **Contact the customer when the action has been completed. Above all, go on selling, building on a new sound, strengthened and revitalised relationship.**

Chapter 3

Professional Selling

In this Chapter:
- **fifteen principles of selling**
- **the selling sequence**
- **the right attitude**
- **necessary knowledge**
- **skills for success.**

Successful selling by phone requires a combination of the right attitudes, skills and knowledge. Basic sales principles apply, but the technique calls for that extra something to help the customer on the other end of the line make the right decisions in your favour.

When we talk about 'professional' in terms of selling, we use it in the same sense as we would when referring to the activity of any other profession or calling. Doctor, vet, architect, solicitor . . . each has attained standards of performance, coupled with experience, which make them a 'professional'. There are no amateurs. We should think of our profession in the same way and be proud of our calling.

> *To be regarded as a professional in your chosen career by your fellow salespeople is the greatest personal achievement to which a salesperson can aspire.*

Selling a product or service over the telephone demands particularly high standards of professionalism. Advantages and benefits have to be impressed upon the listener by words alone, without the help of visual aids.

Is this you?

❓ *I'll give them a ring, although I don't hold out much hopes of an order.*

❓ *I felt a right fool. He knew more than me about our products!*

❓ *Did you know there's a new company muscling in on our territory? I'm blowed if I did!*

❓ *Five calls and no results! I'm fed up.*

Fifteen principles of selling

There's a sure way of recognising a true professional. The pro leaves nothing to chance, plans down to the last detail and adds that extra touch of polished and efficient performance to everything they do. So, run over in your mind how you envisage the dialogue developing between you and a customer.

> *Think in terms of the possible direction – not word for word – the discussion will take. Remain flexible in your attitude and ready to adopt a different approach if necessary.*

Prepare as thoroughly as an actor would for a scene on stage. Have all the facts you're likely to need at hand and be ready for the unexpected query or objection. With experience, after a while you'll find things following a pattern like a familiar script. Instinct will tell you when it's time to change tack and experience will enable you, figuratively speaking, to 'talk on your feet'. Here are some essential principles of selling:

◆ **Enthusiasm**: Without it you'll get nowhere and negate everything you do. Others respond readily to enthusiasm. Let it be unmistakably evident in the tone of your voice and you'll find rapport with your listener is easier to achieve.

♦ **Communication**: At the very heart of selling is the art of gentle persuasion – making someone *want* to do what you want them to do. Make every word and sentence count and ensure that you get your message over and that it is clearly understood.

♦ **Be positive**: This is as essential as enthusiasm. Your speech, thought and action should be directed towards how something can be achieved. Speak with conviction and act confidently as though it's a foregone conclusion that the other person is going to say 'yes'. A listener will very quickly pick up any negative vibes on your part.

♦ **Sincerity**: Always show you're sincere and convince the client that you are trying your best to render them a genuine service.

♦ **Politeness**: You can be polite without being obsequious. The prospective buyer on the other end of the line will be helping you by boosting sales, but don't forget that you're doing them a service in return by letting them in on a good service or product of benefit to them and their business.

◆ **Capture attention**: Aim right from the start to capture – and hold – the attention of a 'prospect'. Plan how you're going to introduce yourself, your company and its products and services in as few words as possible, but with maximum impact.

◆ **The benefits**: Even if you're well aware that the features of your product or service are unique, don't assume a buyer is instantly going to see them as benefits. You have to spell out its characteristics and features in terms of 'what's in it for me?'

◆ **Meeting objections**: Never fear any objections raised by buyers. Dealt with correctly, they add strength to your case. It is better that a customer reveals misgivings which, with the right technique, you can overcome, than you fail to clinch a sale without knowing why. Be ready in advance to answer the more common objections you're most likely to encounter.

◆ **Be a good questioner**: Questions encourage people to talk. Ask structured questions – those beginning with 'what', 'why', 'when', 'how', 'where' and 'who'. It's hard to reply to any of these with a terse 'yes' or 'no'. Usually you'll get answers on which people will feel obliged and pleased to elaborate.

◆ **Be a good listener**: It will pay off to be an attentive listener in return. Customers will be flattered at your obvious interest and you'll add to your knowledge by learning a lot about the person and their business.

◆ **Proof of success**: The fact that you've already successfully sold your product or service to another prestigious or well known company will often secretly impress a prospective customer. It's that ace up your sleeve which could prove a useful sales tool, but one to be used discreetly, particularly where competitors are involved!

◆ **Confirming agreement**: Frequently check to make sure your listener understands what you're saying and agrees with you. Prompts like 'Don't you think so?', 'Isn't that the case?' and 'I hope I've made that clear?' – and that all important 'Do you agree with what we have covered so far – will reveal if there's misunderstanding, lack of conviction or

outright objection on a customer's part.
Remedy them straight away. The more you get a
prospect to say 'yes', the more likely you are to
make sure of that all-important final 'yes'!

◆ **Get a commitment**: Always close a phone call
by getting a commitment from the client.
Ideally, this will be a firm order, but if not, you
should certainly obtain mutual agreement on
what should clearly happen next, whether it's
down to you to act or the buyer. Never be
afraid to ask for this commitment, and confirm
in writing as soon as possible afterwards.

◆ **Plan your work**: Time is money and by
planning your work you could fit additional
phone calls into your schedule. Another selling
call a day equals 250 extra calls a year. Working
on a ratio of successful closes of 1:4, say, you
could be looking at some 62 additional orders!

◆ **Professional development**: Don't neglect your
own development. You have to make definite
progress in your sales career. Be critical of your
own performance – self analysis is necessary to
your continuous self development and the
furtherance of your career.

The selling sequence

The selling process itself breaks down into a sequence of logical stages, from a salesperson's initial planning to final commitment on the customer's part. Fix these steps firmly in mind so that following them through becomes second nature.

◆ Plan before acting. Don't work your way haphazardly through a list of possible clients without first doing some research. Prospect and identify those most likely to yield good business. Think how you're going to introduce yourself and what you're going to say.

◆ Phone the company first to find out the name and title of the person with the buying power (**MAN** – **M**oney/**A**uthority/**N**eed – see p. 44). If you're able speak with them at once, so much the better. If not, make an appointment to phone when they are available.

◆ Once through to the person concerned, introduce yourself and establish that there could be a need for your firm's products or services.

◆ Use structured questions to get information to understand the prospective client's needs and to confirm that you can satisfy those needs.

- ◆ Structured questions will also enable you to establish and explain to the client the major benefits associated with your firm's products or services.

- ◆ 'Thanks, that has helped me understand your needs' is a good way of leading on to a trial close – 'So if . . .' (followed by suggested action).

- ◆ If the prospective customer raises objections at this stage, answer doubts by pointing out and emphasising the benefits.

- ◆ Sell the benefits, obtaining confirmation on these from the prospective customer by 'yes' statements.

- ◆ Close the deal and get commitment.

- ◆ Most important – confirm what has been agreed in writing.

The importance of getting everything in black and white cannot be emphasised enough. Prompt confirmation in writing received the next day gives an indecisive customer less chance to change his or her mind.

The right attitude

An attitude can be defined as a state of mind, a thought process. We're all born with certain attitudes – character traits are part of our personality as an individual. Certain attitudes could hinder our career, but luckily most of us have the chance to improve these and enable us to do our job more effectively. Let's consider some of those attitudes that have a bearing on our success as salespeople:

◆ **Positive and negative**: A positive attitude is healthy and constructive, but a negative one is just plain destructive. The person with a positive attitude tackles a difficult problem by thinking how it can be solved, but the negative-minded person thinks up all the reasons and excuses for not doing anything.

◆ **Determination**: It's no good starting well but finishing badly because you lack the determination to see a thing through to a successful conclusion. Discipline yourself to find a way through any difficulties that threaten to prevent you achieving your objective.

◆ **Taking the initiative**: Although your company may have given you basic training in telesales skills, to be really successful you will still need to be a self-starter, taking the initiative when required and motivating yourself.

◆ **Punctuality**: People with a sloppy attitude towards timekeeping are seen as ineffective and incapable of managing themselves and their time. If you've promised to phone someone at a certain time, keep to it.

◆ **A belief in your profession**: You must be confident in what you do and have an unshakeable belief in the importance of the sales role. Dramatic advances in technology have resulted in manufacturing processes being constantly improved and updated, while computers have revolutionised stock control, office administration and accounting. No one, however, has yet found a better method for the marketing of goods and services than the valuable contribution made by the professional salesperson.

Necessary knowledge

Knowledge is power, and there is certain information relevant to your job that you must make it your first priority to acquire. This does not mean that, having gained this knowledge, you have achieved all that's required. It is only the beginning. The more wide-ranging your knowledge, the better. Having facts at your fingertips on a variety of subjects allied to selling and marketing in general will give you confidence and demonstrate to a prospective customer that you really know what you are talking about. Essential knowledge falls into four main subjects:

◆ **Products or services**: You must be thoroughly familiar with your company's entire range of products or services, so that you can discuss them knowledgeably and without hesitation.

*Aside from factual and technical details, you must be able to present the various features in terms of benefits to a prospective buyer. **Remember: sell the benefits***.

◆ **Your company**: For your own information and that of customers who ask you, it's useful to know the history and background of your firm and any associated companies. As an employee you should be aware of its policies, procedures and know the names of key personnel and what they do.

◆ **The competition**: Know the opposition – competitors in the same field and their products. Set up your own market intelligence to monitor their activity. Trade magazines and finance columns in the newspapers are worth scanning. Often existing or prospective customers will let slip information about a rival you can follow up discreetly.

◆ **Your target market**: The products or services you're selling are bound to impose their own restrictions when, for example, delivery and technical back-up are taken into consideration. Start with an area in mind and concentrate on exploiting it to the full before looking for opportunities for expansion further afield.

Skills for success

Your skills are the means by which you bring into action the right attitudes and high levels of knowledge you have developed and acquired. These skills are vital to success in telesales, where by voice alone you have to persuade customers to commit themselves.

♦ First and foremost is **good communication** – the art of conveying information accurately and succinctly to others. You are just as much in the communication business as anyone working in advertising, publishing or broadcasting.

♦ **Articulate speech**: You must use language as imaginatively and persuasively as possible to sell an idea. Creating favourable word pictures in your listener's mind will help you to sell the product or service.

♦ **Listening intelligently**: A professional salesperson is a good listener as well as a good talker. And by asking questions, structured questions, requiring definite answers gets people to talk about their company, its business and its needs – all plus points when it comes to closing an interview with an action decision.

♦ **Overcoming objections**: This necessary skill will come with practice and experience. As well as having a ready answer to any of the 'standard' objections a prospective client is likely to raise, you must be prepared to deal decisively and convincingly with any others.

◆ **Closing sales calls**: How you close a phone conversation with a buyer is all important. Ideally you will have achieved the sale, but if not, you must get the buyer to agree to an 'action decision'.

Make sure that both you and the customer are quite clear about what happens next, such as further moves on your part or the buyer's.

◆ **Effective use of time**: Discipline yourself to make every minute count. Aim to get in as many telesales calls a day as are practicable and allocate the time accordingly. Experience will tell you in advance which calls are likely to take up more time than others.

◆ **Self-management**: This involves setting yourself objectives for achieving or bettering the sales revenue targets you have been set by management. Constantly monitor your progress towards gaining your goals and hitting your sales targets!

In summary...

◆ Be a true professional and have unshakeable
 pride in the role salespeople play in.

◆ Adopt the right attitude to the job. Always be
 positive – never negative – in your dealings
 with customers.

◆ Let your knowledge about your company's
 products and services be second to none.

◆ Know your competitors and keep abreast of the
 latest developments in your particular field.

◆ Be an articulate communicator and a good
 listener.

Chapter 4

Buying Motives

In this Chapter:
- **six primary motivations to buy**
- **understanding the buyer's motivation**
- **personality of the buyer**
- **recognition with the appropriate response.**

To buy or not to buy – that is the question. People have various motives or reasons for buying products or services, and one particular reason will always be foremost. If you understand these motives and the pattern of selling resulting from them, you have the key to the whole art of selling.

Before we go into the buying and selling process, let's first be quite clear what we mean by the term 'buyer'. Whether the person you're contacting by phone is already an existing customer or a prospective one, they must have:

- ◆ Access to **M**oney to pay for your product or service.

- ◆ The **A**uthority to go ahead and order from you.

- ◆ A **N**eed for your particular product or service.

> *Remembered easily as MAN. If you haven't checked on the credentials of your contact by discreet inquiries beforehand, do so as soon as possible. Otherwise, you could find you have wasted your time talking to the wrong person.*

Your customer may not necessarily be the conventional buyer – the person who issues the right paperwork and signs the order. On occasions, for instance, you could find yourself dealing with the works manager, production engineer or even the managing director.

> *MAN is overridden when a proprietorial decision maker is involved to give final approval.*

It's important to remember, too, that often today's buying decisions are not made by one person but by a committee of people. Think of them as a decision making unit (DMU). Each DMU member

is likely to have ideas, motivations and needs
differing from the others, particularly when it's a
multi-stage sale.

Is this you?

❓ *I know the price is competitive, I wish I knew
the thinking behind their decision not to buy.*

❓ *How can I convince their buyer that they have a
real need for our service?*

❓ *I've tried every trick in the book to get the sale,
but it's still no go.*

❓ *Just when I think I'm about to clinch the deal,
he draws back from making a definite
commitment. What am I doing wrong?*

Six primary motivations to buy

In any decision to buy, one buyer's reasons for
buying or not buying will be different from
another's. Reasons can be divided into:

◆ rational ones where straightforward logic and
business sense play their part

◆ emotional reasons arising from the buyer's personal preferences or feelings at any particular time.

Sometimes the two come into conflict, for example, with the buyer appreciating the value of a product or service to their company, but uncertain about the actual benefits. Business reasons come into play where a product or service is of benefit to the buyer's business, whereas personal reasons are involved when the benefit is likely to be to the buyer alone.

> *It's often difficult to discover the hidden emotional and personal reasons for buyers' decisions, but what we do know is that intelligence or reason plays a significant role in determining the outcome.*

Rational reasons for buying are more important as far as you, the seller is concerned. You can present the facts about your product or service with no beating about the bush, but appealing to the buyer's emotional reasons has to be done with finesse. A direct approach could well embarrass the buyer – none of us likes to discuss how we personally feel. Asking the buyer structured, open-ended questions – the kind that require an answer, not a blunt 'yes' or 'no' – will give you clues about how the buyer thinks and feels.

The six primary motivations for buying are:

♦ **Safety and security**: Those paid to make buying decisions are very conscious of their vulnerability. They know they will be judged by their bosses on whether they tend to make more good decisions than wrong ones. Every time they spend the company's money they risk their personal reputation. As well as making the right decision financially, the buyer also wants assurance that they're doing business with a company that's sound, and whether the product or service itself is sound.

♦ **Performance and efficiency**: A buyer also looks for good all-round performance including consistent quality, satisfactory value, reliable back-up service and prompt advice if needed. As the salesperson it's your job to assure the buyer on all counts.

♦ **Appearance and novelty**: Exciting changes in packaging and presentation mean that many products have taken on a new and attractive appearance. There is no doubt that the novelty of new shapes and colours capture the imagination of buyers.

♦ **Convenience and comfort**: A good sales point is to emphasise how easy it is to do business with you and your company, with a maintenance and back-up service second to none and advice readily available when required. Anything in your telesales pitch which demonstrates how the day-to-day working life of everyone concerned can be made easier will be welcome news to your listeners.

♦ **Economy and right price**: Economies are made in two forms – money and effort. Everything comes down to money in the end. Financial savings are effected by carrying out the same operation for less cost or chalking up a gain by getting more done for the same or slightly more cost. Economies of effort are made by getting the same work done for less effort, or the gain resulting from more getting done for the same effort. Add up all the gains and savings from money and effort and you arrive at the right price.

> *We use the term 'effort' in this context in preference to 'labour'.*

◆ **Durability and dependability:** This motive for buying is a question of how long a product or service will continue to give the buyer the benefits for which it was originally bought.

> *Durability in another sense is also a consideration when a prospective buyer looks to the future and wants reassurance that the seller's company can continue to maintain standards and give the type of service required if they go ahead.*

Understanding the buyer's motivation

Other factors that can affect the successful conclusion of a deal include:

◆ The amount of money available from the budget.

◆ The cost of your product or service compared with those of others.

- The benefits your product or service offers against alternatives.

- The technical specification of the product.

- Improved service performance.

The evaluation of these factors and the importance placed on them by the buyer varies from individual to individual. A works manager, for example, will listen to the facts from the practical production point of view, while the accountant will be more concerned about the financial return on the investment. You must therefore take this into account when planning your strategy.

Personality of the buyer

You might think of those buying your firm's product or service on behalf of their companies as being more rational than actual consumers. But they're only human like the rest of us. Emotional factors can affect rational thought on someone's part. Some examples are:

- The mood the buyer is in at that particular moment. Perhaps your timing is unfortunate – they could be facing a business or domestic crisis.

- The working relationship between two or more people in a company jointly involved in the decision making where there is a clash of personalities between individuals.

- The regard or otherwise in which the buyer holds your company, judging its reputation or standing from personal experience or from others' opinions.

- The source of the referral or recommendation, particularly if friendship or family is involved.

- The personal reaction to you as the seller. If adverse, this could cause the buyer to distort or reject the facts you present them with and seriously jeopardise your chances of a sale.

This underlies how important it is to impress a potential buyer with a polished, professional telesales pitch.

- Pressure from others demanding the buyer's time or attention.

- The extent of the buyer's own background knowledge and experience.

- The newness or novelty of your product or service as described by you or contained in sales literature already sent.

- 'Value for money' as perceived by the buyer.

- And you can't rule out the possibility of the buyer feeling unwell and losing concentration.

Recognition with the appropriate response

By listening intently you will come to sense when emotional factors are involved and take them into account in your approach. Ask the buyer those structured open-ended questions, get them talking, giving you clues about what they're thinking and feeling.

As we've seen, the art of selling is to recognise and identify each customer's motives for buying – what in effect turns their interest on. Then it's a question of directing your tactics to appeal to the buyer. Tailor your whole style and manner of approach to suit. For example:

- If they're very status conscious, stress benefits like 'the latest design just out'.

◆ Where security is uppermost in the buyer's mind, reassure them by emphasising benefits like the guarantee or reliable back-up service.

◆ If the buyer is hesitant, reassure them, be friendly with those who like an informal approach, and be respectful but not obsequious to the more formal person.

More subtle personality traits, such as the following examples, should be taken into account:

◆ **Freudian**: There's the person, irrespective of age and gender, who likes to be seen as having a dominant personality. Such a buyer will try to call the shots during your telesales chat with them. Here your strategy will be to let them think they're in charge, while subtly directing the conversation your way.

In complete contrast there is the person who considers themselves to be essentially gentle and artistic. They will concentrate more on colour and design and let you do most of the running.

◆ **Relationships**: Some buyers like to cultivate and maintain friendly relationships with business contacts. They will aim to keep you happy – and, probably, your competitors, too!

◆ **Ambitions**: Every person has ambitions, and a buyer in a company is ambitious to be even more successful in the eyes of superiors and colleagues. You must aim at convincing an ambitious person that buying your product or service on behalf of their company will enhance their reputation for decisive action and shrewd business acumen.

◆ **Prejudices**: Hearsay, gossip and even the media play a part in creating and fanning the flames of personal prejudices. Where you sense prejudice on the part of a buyer, tread carefully.

◆ **Fears**: If you sense a buyer has a number of concerns, carefully play on the ones that could be to your advantage – like the very real fear of missing out on something good, for instance. But don't overstress the virtues of your product or service to the extent that the buyer then starts to fear they're being taken for a ride and being stampeded into making the wrong buying decision.

It's all down to you developing an empathy with the person on the other end of the line – being in tune with how they feel and act. Like us all, buyers will try to conceal what they are and how they think. No buyer is going to come out in the open and help you in your sales pitch by confessing if they're greedy, mean and vain. It's up to you to look, listen and work out the best way to approach each individual. It's a challenge, and part of the enjoyment of being a good telesales person.

In summary...

◆ In each company you approach, identify the person who has the buying power, authority to spend and a need for your product or service.

◆ Understand the motivation for buying and how it differs according to individuals and their role in a company.

◆ Learn to empathise with the buyer and discover what makes them tick.

◆ Adapt your sales strategy according to what you have been able to find out about the buyer's personality, their needs and those of their company.

Chapter 5

Clear Communication

In this Chapter:

- **transmitting a clear message**
- **nine pointers to better communication**
- **open questions**
- **starter phrases.**

Communication can be defined as the interchange of thoughts, opinions, ideas or information by speech or writing. A professional salesperson must have the expertise to communicate ideas effectively with others, for without this essential skill good ideas or vital information will be lost. This is particularly important when it comes to telesales work.

You won't be able to communicate effectively if you:

- neglect to listen to what the other person is saying

- over react to the comments and views of others

- obstinately refuse to see another point of view

- refuse to accept that other people are entitled to their views and opinions.

You don't always need to agree, but you must recognise that the needs of others are as valid as your own.

Before you go into your sales routine, aim first to build up a relationship or rapport with the customer. The skills you use to achieve this are basically the same as you employ socially when establishing relationships outside work. This involves:

- respect for the other person

- understanding for their point of view

- being yourself – honest and sincere.

Establishing relationships, building rapport with others, or selling are not skills we are born with – they have to be developed and practised. As a professional, to build a rapport you must first show you are genuine and that you respect and understand your customers.

> *It's not enough for you to feel this – you've got to communicate it as well. People are not mind readers. They can only hear what you're saying over the telephone.*

Taking the trouble to remember a person's name, and perhaps such details as family interests or hobbies, help to make your customer feel important – it's a way of showing them respect. Tuning in to what a person feels as well as what they say and responding to it shows that you understand. Keeping promises, being truthful and admitting when you are in the wrong or have made mistakes show that you are genuine and intend to be yourself.

When tuning in on their wavelength, make sure that they're really taking in what you have to say and haven't 'switched off'. Without the advantage of speaking with them face to face, this will require careful listening and questioning on your part to check they are responding.

Is this you?

❓ *I believe in coming straight to the point – do they or don't they want to buy?*

❓ *I can't be bothered with all that 'How's the family?' nonsense.*

❓ *Their buyer got entirely the wrong end of the stick.*

❓ *Everyone's entitled to their own opinion, provided it agrees with mine.*

❓ *OK, so I'll be understanding and friendly, but I don't have to be close mates with the guy.*

Transmitting a clear message

However good you are as a communicator, you will come into contact with many people who are not. Experts tell us that we speak at about 150 to 200 words a minute, but can grasp ideas at some 10 times that rate. Any telesales message we transmit must be interesting enough to capture your listener's attention. Every message sent contains at least four meanings:

◆ What you *mean to say*.

- What you *actually say.*

- What the listener *hears.*

- What the listener *thinks they hear.*

Just think of the number of times you've heard people say, 'That's not what I meant' or 'That's what I understood you to say'. We all have difficulty in expressing our thoughts so that others can interpret them correctly.

So when you are on the telephone to a customer telling them about your product or service:

- Don't hurry. Avoid gabbling and make sure every word is heard by your listener.

- Speak clearly, giving impact to your words.

> *By doing so you will feel more confident, which in turn will inspire confidence in the customer.*

- Be economical with words and never use a long one where a short one will do just as well. Find words that best express the qualities of your product or service.

◆ Speak of your product with respect. By doing so you will accord it the importance it deserves in the listener's eyes.

◆ Don't be too formal. By speaking conversationally you put things on a more friendly basis, become more persuasive and lessen the possibility of tension developing between you and the customer.

◆ And put that smile in your voice. It will reduce any possible tension, encourage the customer and indicate your willingness to help and please.

While delivering your sales message, do listen carefully and respond to any comments from your listener. Until the day when technology enables us to see the person we're phoning, the disadvantage of telesales is not being able to observe and read another's body language. So note every hesitation, change of tone and nuance, as well as listening intelligently to what your listener has to say.

Nine pointers to better communication

1 **Reflect success**: You're the salesperson claiming to represent a successful company – right? So

be positive, confident, assured – project through your voice an equally successful image of yourself.

> *Make sure the way you come over to your listener reflects that success and mirrors the confidence you have in your company and its services and products. Get into character right away!*

2 **Points of order**: You know what you are talking about, but is the customer as clearly in the picture? Make what you're trying to get across easier to follow by presenting each point or idea in an orderly logical sequence. And keep on the straight and narrow – it's all too easy to stray from the main theme.

3 **Ring the vocal changes**: Vary your tone to avoid your voice becoming monotonous. Develop a pleasant tone, and pitch your voice at just the right level to ensure every word you utter is heard and understood. Show enthusiasm to emphasise or strengthen the points you make.

4 **Be persuasive**: When it comes to influencing others to change their views or cherished

beliefs, take a leaf out of Aristotle's book. The wise old Greek identified what he called the three essential pillars of persuasion as fact, emotion and credibility:

- *Fact* – arrange and deliver your facts in rational order.

- *Emotion* – stir your listener to want to make changes and accept new ideas from you.

- *Credibility* – get your listener to believe in you. Once you have credibility, they'll accept what you have to say about any product or service.

5 **Use 'you' appeal**: Use 'you' not 'I' for all you're worth. However scintillating your sales pitch, it will fail to impress if it's not immediately obviously of personal interest to listeners. And give your listener a chance to talk about themselves. Follow Benjamin Disraeli's tip: 'Talk to a man about himself and he will listen for hours.'

6 **Stimulate the brain**: Communication is a two-way process. You want your listener to react positively to what you are saying. Think of ways to stimulate their brain, and you're in business. One surefire way of doing this is to ask your

listener's advice or opinion – questions they just can't wait to answer. Show a genuine interest and make them feel important.

> *And for your part listen carefully to what they have to say. Be a good listener as well as a good talker – and make notes as you go along.*

7 **Avoid bias of any sort**: It's all too easy to stereotype, label or generalise about any person or group. Accept, too, that people are more than likely to label you. And their impressions will determine if they're going to accept or reject what you tell them. Don't blow it by making careless comments that could offend or hurt the person on the end of the line.

8 **Empathise**: Always put yourself in the other person's place. Try to think and feel like them. Only when you empathise with them can you fully appreciate their needs and tailor your message accordingly in a way that promises to fulfil them. Courtesy and sincerity are sure winners at all times.

9 **Over-communicating**: Say your piece, then finish. Don't try to be too clever, don't overdo

the detail, don't repeat yourself or waffle. In the end, quality not quantity is what you'll be judged on. Don't leave the customer confused and punch drunk, having missed the salient points you've been trying to put over.

KISS is the golden rule: Keep It Short and Sweet, Or to drive the point home, Keep It Short, Stupid!

Open questions

You can invariably tell a good telesales person from a poor one by the way they use skilful questioning techniques. Many salespeople who otherwise have a sound knowledge of their company and its products or services fail to clearly identify the buyer's needs. All too often they just present the benefits without establishing the buyer's requirements.

Open questions are structured questions that prompt informative replies from the buyer, which give you, the seller, a sound base on which to present a product or service directed towards specific customer need.

Start questions with:

◆ What . . . ?
◆ Which . . . ?
◆ Why . . . ?
◆ Where . . . ?
◆ When . . . ?
◆ To what extent/degree . . . ?
◆ How . . . ?

and you'll be able to draw out information on which to build a sales pitch to match the defined individual needs of the customer.

Don't use weaker openings such as:

◆ Shall . . .?
◆ Will . . . ?
◆ Can . . . ?
◆ Are . . . ?
◆ Would . . . ?
◆ Should . . . ?
◆ Could . . . ?
◆ May . . . ?
◆ Ought . . . ?
◆ Might . . . ?
◆ Is . . . ?

Closed questions are those that begin with:

◆ Do you . . . ?
◆ Can you . . . ?
◆ Are you . . . ?

and so on. The answer is almost always a non-committal 'yes' or flat 'no', which gives you no information or feedback. There is, of course, always an exception. You're allowed to ask just one closed or unstructured question and that's 'Can I have the business?' In this case a 'yes' is OK – very acceptable!

Starter phrases

Here are examples of open or structured questions:

◆ How important is it to you that . . . ?

◆ What importance would you place on . . . ?

◆ How much an advantage to you would it be if . . . ?

◆ We are able to provide . . . How useful would you find that?

- What is this problem costing you?

- How do you think you'll solve it?

- How much money has been allocated to solving this problem?

- How did you reach this figure?

- When will the money be available?

- If we can come up with a significantly better answer of slightly more than the figure budgeted, would you consider it?

- How much happier would you be knowing that . . . ?

- How much more impressed would you be if . . . ?

- Why do you say that?

- How much more credibility would you have if . . . ?

- To what extent does . . . ?

- What extra results could you get if . . . ?

And during your telephone conversation, take the opportunity to find out discreetly who your competitors are and get an idea of their strengths and weaknesses with questions like:

- Which other suppliers are you in discussion with?

- Have you used any of these suppliers before?

- Who decides which supplier gets the order?

- Which supplier do you favour at this stage?

And if it's one of your competitors, follow it up with: Why?

In summary...

- **Tune in to the listener and establish a rapport before the sales pitch.**
- **Make sure what you mean to say coincides with what you actually say.**
- **Speak clearly and make sure every word is heard by your listener.**
- **Listen carefully and respond to any comments from a customer.**
- **Identify the buyer's needs with open and structured questions.**
- **Keep your message short, sweet and on track.**

Chapter 6

Outgoing Calls

In this Chapter:
- ◆ **objectives of telemarketing**
- ◆ **preparation and planning**
- ◆ **achieving objectives**
- ◆ **planning the call**
- ◆ **guarding against time wasting**
- ◆ **getting through to the decision maker**
- ◆ **making appointments on the phone.**

The volume of business conducted over the telephone is ever increasing. It accounts for a large percentage of the turnover of suppliers of products and services. Efficient telemarketing saves time, effort and money for both supplier and customer. Indeed, prime customer target groups have become well accustomed to this form of contact with suppliers.

We phone people because it saves time. Used skilfully the telephone is a very quick way for us to sound out a prospective customer. If they fulfil the criteria of **MAN** (access to **M**oney, **A**uthority to order from you and a **N**eed for your company's product or service) you can make an appointment to present your case and secure a sale.

> *A professional telesales plan closely linked to sales representative activity can dramatically increase the cost effectiveness of the salesforce.*

Many salespeople shy away from using the phone to make appointments. They are perhaps daunted by having to overcome obstructive switchboard operators and personal secretaries to get to the person they're phoning. They think, too, that it's all too easy for a customer to put them off and refuse to meet them. A professional salesperson should look upon these as challenges and apply the right techniques to overcome them.

Is this you?

❓ *Planning and preparation? I play each phone call by ear.*

❓ *I've given up trying to make contact – the switchboard always fobs me off.*

❓ *I spent a lot of time briefing his secretary and now she tells me he's not interested.*

❓ *OK, so I wasn't being quite truthful, but now and then you have to bluff a little.*

❓ *How do you get past the secretary? I've left messages, but obviously the boss isn't getting them*

Objectives of telemarketing

Like any sales approach there have to be objectives. You must plan the call and control the interview. This is even more important in telephone selling than in face-to-face selling. Remember, on your initial contact by phone you are not just selling the product or service, you are selling an appointment and qualifying a prospect. Why should the customer agree to meet with you?

A good salesperson uses a device called a 'hook'. The hook is the reason for the customer granting you an interview. So when you start to build your telephone strategy, keep in mind your objectives and remember to put a hook into the conversation very early. Other objectives of telemarketing include:

◆ Quotation follow-up calls.

◆ Promotional follow-ups.

◆ Test marketing.

◆ New product launches.

◆ Representative call scheduling.

◆ Making customers aware of special events.

Telemarketing also involves dealing with incoming queries and requests:

◆ Response to company advertising.

◆ Taking orders over the phone.

◆ Problem solving.

◆ Literature requests.

◆ Customer services.

Preparation and planning

Planning involves determining what should be done, by whom and when, in order to achieve predetermined objectives. Using your time wisely to work for you is the essence of good planning, which has a vital part to play in good selling. And good selling is the means by which you're going to achieve financial rewards and progression in your chosen career. Set yourself specific goals, then decide:

◆ how you plan to carry them out

◆ what will be the timescale to enable you to achieve each goal.

The salesperson with a carefully thought out plan can achieve any goal or ambition more easily and more quickly than one with an ill conceived plan, or worse, none at all.

> *Prioritise according to the most or least value a call is likely to yield in money or future business.*

◆ No one plans to fail, but many fail to plan! Be
  SMART – plan the work and work the plan:

  – **S**chedule your time, because without a
    schedule you could become sloppy and
    waste time unnecessarily.

  – **M**ake time and ensure every minute counts.
    Even when you're not talking to a customer,
    you should be spending time productively.

  – **A**llow yourself sufficient time. Never
    underestimate the amount of time it takes
    to do a thorough selling job on a buyer,
    especially a prospective one. Don't have a
    timetable so tight and inflexible that your
    whole day's telemarketing programme could
    be wrecked by something unforeseen
    turning up.

  – **R**ation time effectively. Most of your time
    ought to be devoted to what look to be the
    most profitable existing or potential clients.

  – **T**ake your time. Don't rush things and take
    whatever time you need to clinch a sale.

Achieving objectives

When setting objectives make them specific, so

that progress towards them can be accurately measured. They should be independent of each other, so that you can be quite clear in your mind what action is needed for achieving individual objectives.

Your second step is to establish a priority for each objective. Step three should be to determine how you will know you have successfully achieved an objective in terms of performance and results. These should be mutually agreed with your sales manager.

Objectives can be long or short term. With the former you're obviously looking well ahead. Sometimes it's necessary to achieve a long-term objective by a series of linked short-term ones. No matter what the objectives you set yourself – increased sales, self development, more efficient customer service, streamlining and overhaul of office systems – constantly check and monitor your progress on each.

Planning the call

You will have a list of objectives, too, when

making a telesales call. The difference between the professional salesperson and the amateur is quite marked when a sales call is being planned. A good professional keeps in mind the law of maximum and minimum returns – the most or least value the call is likely to yield. In other words, the good salesperson does not put the receiver down after a call without having achieved something.

Before making a call, think out what you're going to say. Rehearse everything mentally from start to finish. Think of the possible objections a prospective buyer is likely to raise and work out how you're going to answer them. Then ask yourself what is the maximum you expect from your telephone call. Set a value on it, if you can. The figure could be in monetary terms or in the volume you hope to sell, but you must keep it in your mind as the target to strive for during the call.

Where you think there's only a fifty-fifty chance of making a sale, set yourself not only a maximum figure, but an intermediate figure and a minimum one. You'll have added confidence and the psychological advantage of not worrying whether or not you're going to get the business. Assume that you're going to be successful and that it's only a matter of just how much business you're going to get.

Now set yourself an intermediate figure. If you don't get all of the business, what will you aim for next? Perhaps you'll try for half the business now (as a secondary/back-up supplier), and hope to build on this in the future. You then have to decide the minimum you're prepared to accept at the end of the call, if you don't make first base with your maximum and minimum target levels. For example, this could take the form of persuading a buyer to accept a trial purchase, which you're confident will later lead to increased firm orders.

> *But make every effort to succeed at the top level. Only move down the scale after you have given it your best shots. Never accept less where there's a chance to exact the maximum.*

When rehearsing the telesales call, think of the process like this:

♦ **Objective**: Establish the specific reason for your call in measurable terms. Get it quite clear in your mind what you intend persuading the buyer or prospective buyer to do.

◆ **Openers**: Friendly conversation at the beginning of your sales pitch will put your listener at ease. Concentrate on making statements that capture the buyer's attention, create interest and arouse curiosity.

◆ **Added client profile information**: By using open questions you will add necessary additional qualifying information you've been unable to obtain prior to your call, especially as regards needs and problems.

◆ **Description of product or service**: Here is where your real sales pitch begins and you present all the features of your product or service

◆ **Benefits to the buyer**: You have to sell the benefits that result from using your product or service, whether it's solving problems, reducing costs, making the job easier, simplifying the operation or, on a personal level, increasing the buyer's income or giving them kudos in the eyes of their colleagues or company.

◆ **The close**: Give serious thought to possible methods of closing. Have you the determination to get a decision for action to be taken on something, either by you or the customer? Is your diary at hand for the follow-up call? Are you ready to record details of the call, so that at the end you can critically analyse your performance and see if it all went as you intended?

Guarding against time wasting

Everyone has 24 hours a day available at their disposal, but most people don't use the time wisely. They fritter it away mainly because they've never really thought about how they could benefit by converting their available time.

Time wasters include unnecessary paperwork, appointments running over time and refreshment breaks.

> *Remember KISS and Keep It Short and Sweet.*

Paperwork should be left until the end of the day and completed either at home in the evening or when you have completed your list of calls for the day. Coffee breaks and lunches are necessary – no one should go without food and drink – but don't get into the habit of extended breaks. Keep your lunchtime short and use the period to call customers before or after they have their lunch. Lunchtimes can be a good period of the day in which to call buyers. Don't impose on their lunchtime, but at the same time don't write off the lunch period altogether. It is possible to plan appointments between noon and 2pm.

Letting a call drag on – often because of idle discussion – will also lose you precious minutes. Once you've made the sale, or reached some form of commitment, politely hang up. Chatting on unnecessarily not only wastes time – it could irritate your listener and endanger all you have achieved.

Plan your telemarketing weekly and daily, listing the calls and giving priority to those which you consider offer you the most potential business. Say you'll ring back if a decision maker's line is engaged, don't just hang on. Then move swiftly on to your next prospect.

Getting through to the decision maker

When you make a phone call, getting through to the person who has **MAN**:

- access to Money to pay for your product or service

- the Authority to go ahead and order from you

- a Need for your particular product or service

is not always simple. Switchboard operators and secretaries are often instructed not to put calls through directly from salespeople. Here are ways by which you as a professional salesperson can overcome obstructions like these.

First of all, it's always advisable when speaking to the switchboard to ask the operator right away for the name of the person responsible for buying and ask to be put through. If the operator questions you as to who you are, where you are from and why you want to speak to him or her, always answer truthfully. The secret is not to make your answer brief and to the point. Go into some detail and 'dress it up' when giving your reason for wishing to speak to the person responsible for buying. The chances are your explanation could prove a little too complicated for the operator to remember and pass on all the facts, in which case you'll be put straight through. It's also likely that by the time you've finished explaining, things will be hotting up on the switchboard as other callers start ringing in and the operator will be unable to afford spending any more precious minutes dealing with you.

Use the same technique if you get a similar reception from a secretary protecting their boss from what they think are unnecessary callers. Always remain cool and polite, after all, they're only doing their job. Never let yourself be encouraged into discussing your company's products or services with a switchboard operator or a secretary. And don't be content to leave a message with a helpful secretary either, however much they faithfully promise to pass it on.

Your opening gambit when through to the buyer's secretary should be along these lines:

> 'May I speak to Mr Severn?'

Secretary: 'What is it about?'

> 'Oh, isn't he there? Could you tell me what time you expect him back, please?'

Secretary: 'Oh, he is here, but he's in a meeting.

Can I help?'

Well, it's a little complicated. I need some information from him. Would it be better if I called back this afternoon or tomorrow morning?'

If you give away all the facts about your company's products or services right at the start, it's very easy for a customer briefed by their secretary to give you a straight 'no' or misinterpret the facts and tell you they don't think it's suitable.

When you do get through to the decision maker, adopt a businesslike but pleasant manner:

◆ introduce yourself
◆ state your company name
◆ give a brief description of your firm.

Then

◆ build a bridge and establish a rapport

◆ sound them out to get a feedback of relevant facts to enable you to determine issues and problems and offer solutions

◆ close for an appointment.

Making appointments on the phone

The telephone has proved its value as a medium for making appointments in terms of time and effort. To get you relaxed and comfortable, let's run over the essentials for successfully getting that telesales appointment:

◆ First of all, be comfortably seated and relaxed. It might seem basic common sense, but you'd be surprised at the number of people who attempt to make a call standing up or leaning over a desk. If right-handed, holding the telephone in your left hand leaves you free to write.

◆ Have ready to hand all the things you will need, for example, your diary, a calendar, a note pad, and information you have so far on the prospective buyer's company – plus pen or pencil.

◆ Place in front of you an outline script of how you think the call will progress. Include on it all stages of contact from the switchboard onwards.

◆ Write answers to all likely objections raised against granting an appointment.

◆ Prepare at least three different closes. Everyone has their favourite close, but you don't want to overdo one technique.

◆ Practise the script with a colleague, using your internal telephone system.

◆ Learn to paraphrase your script. Don't read it out, but highlight key phrases and build what you have to say around them.

When making the call, smile and let that smile show in your voice. It's worth again stressing the following points:

◆ Take care not to speak too fast and articulate carefully in well-modulated tones.

◆ If you don't know the name of the buyer, get their name from the switchboard before asking to be connected.

◆ When connected to a secretary or assistant who asks the purpose of your call, give a brief explanation in general terms, then ask politely, but firmly to be put through to the person you want. If they are not available, find out when they'll be free and say you'll ring back then.

Once through to the customer in person, state your name and that of your company at once. If appropriate, ask them whether they know your company or your products. This will get the buyer talking early, but will not affect your control of the conversation. Whenever possible tell them you know something about their business or their needs and problems. If you don't have the full picture sound them out.

Following on from this:

◆ Suggest in general terms that you have something of interest to them, but don't make positive claims and never go into detail. It's much too early and you might get unwanted objections.

If you have planned your call properly, you will have anticipated likely objections and be prepared to overcome them. Another ploy is: 'That's one of the points I hope we can discuss when we meet.' Then close for the appointment. Objections to granting an appointment should be acknowledged politely, using the 'Yes, but . . .' technique, followed by close.

- Don't pressure the buyer. Speak slowly and surely, and plan to pause at points where they are unlikely to interrupt and take control.

- Remember you are selling an appointment – not a product or service at this stage. So close as soon as you possibly can – often within the first minute.

- Your first close should be general, such as 'I'd like to come and see you next week. Are mornings or afternoons more convenient?'

- On getting a positive response, fix the appointment immediately.

- Make appointments for 15-minute periods – 10.15 or 2.30 suggests you are precise, busy, punctual and brief.

- Confirm the appointment, repeating the time and date clearly and slowly, telling them you are writing it in your diary.

- Thank them and say goodbye.

Here are two typical examples of getting an appointment:

Greet and identify	'Good morning, Mr South. My name is Felix Severn. I'm from XYZ.'
Get buyer to speak	'Are you familiar with our products/services?'
If no	'Then may I tell you that . . .'
If yes	'Then you may know that . . .'
Gain interest	'We make . . . and we have a new range which I think may be of interest to your company. I would very much like to show it to you. Perhaps we could meet one day next week?' *or* 'We have a new range which we believe is far more reliable in industries like yours. How important is reliability to you at present?'
If important	'Then I'd very much like you to see the range . . .'
If not	'Well, the range has several other features which I think could save you money in other

areas and I'd very much like to meet you and show you how. . .'
or

'We've never met, Mr South, and I'd very much like to put that right and show you some of our products. Could we fix a time one day next week?'

'Mr South, I understand that your company . . . (state any known fact that implies a possible need for your product or service)

'We have a product/service that I believe might be of interest to you and I'd appreciate the opportunity to discuss it. I shall be in Newton on . . .'

Establish best time 'Tell me, Mr South, are mornings or afternoons more convenient?'

Make appointment 'Fine. How about Friday? I can make 9.15. Or would Thursday at 9.45 suit you better?'

Confirm	'Thanks, Mr South, I'm making a note in my diary. Friday, the 7th, at 9.15. I look forward to meeting you.'

In summary...

- ◆ Good planning results in good selling. Plan the work, then work the plan.
- ◆ Observe the law of maximum and minimum returns and prioritise calls according to value.
- ◆ Deal only with the decision maker and concentrate on selling the appointment not the product or service.

Chapter 7

Sell! Sell! Sell!

In this Chapter:

◆ **selling on the telephone**
◆ **selling benefits**
◆ **overcoming objections**
◆ **closing the sale**
◆ **the follow-up call.**

This is where you put theory into practice, where everything covered so far about the principles of successful telesales and telemarketing falls into place. Confident in yourself, your company and in the product or service you are selling, you need only a few final pointers to add the finishing touches to a successful sales technique.

People buy what they want. It may be a truism, but unless you find out what a customer wants you'll get nowhere right from the start. It's no good assuming you know what it is they are looking for, without them actually telling you. Gathering intelligence and background information on the company you're targeting beforehand will give you some idea, so that you're not operating completely 'blind'. It's as well to find out, too, what the particular purchasing set-up is.

> *Will you be dealing with an individual decision maker with MAN, for instance, or a buyer who has to get permission from someone else?*

By skilful questioning during the actual telesales call you will be able to fill in the gaps in your knowledge and build up a complete profile of the company and its requirements. You can also gain an insight into what makes the particular buyer 'tick', which will give you a psychological advantage, increased confidence and help you determine what your sales strategy will be. Once you have established the need, then you can start the selling and persuasion.

Is this you?

❓ *Cut them short when they go on about their company's business, I say.*

❓ *I'm always uncertain about when I should try to close a deal.*

❓ *Well, how was I to know that objection would be sprung on me?*

❓ *Couldn't get a word in edgeways from the moment he picked up the phone.*

❓ *Too late I realised that I wasn't familiar with his company and I think it showed.*

Selling on the telephone

Selling is essentially a two-phase process. Phase one is to find out what the prospective customer wants by what is known as probing. What you find out is known as the 'hot button', because the selling process really gets going when you make contact with it in phase two. Phase two is where you match what product or service you are offering to that hot button by means of your sales pitch or presentation.

The structure for all telesales contact is:

◆ **Probe** – questioning a prospect to find out their wants or needs.

◆ **Confirm** – establishing what those wants or needs are (the hot button).

◆ **Match** – lining up what you have to offer with the hot button.

◆ **Close** – achieving a firm commitment regarding action to be taken either immediately or at an agreed date in the future.

The probe must essentially be a conversation – not a question and answer session. By being enthusiastic, showing interest in the prospect's business and mainly using open-ended questions, you can prompt the prospect to talk about their business. If your probing is skilful enough, the prospect should be hardly aware that you are asking him questions at all.

Remember that this should be informal and friendly. Avoid it becoming an interrogation at all costs.

Just as people like talking about themselves and their family, business people like talking about their firm and their business. But it is your job to guide and control the conversation throughout. Don't let the prospect's enthusiasm run away with

them! Make most of your questions open-ended –
What? Why? When? How? Where? Who? – so that
the prospect has to volunteer information instead
of just answering 'yes' or 'no'.

To get the conversation started and generate a
high level of interest use a 'hook' after you have
introduced yourself. This is a general statement
which gives the prospect a reason for your call and
leads gently into the opening hot button statement.

> *Many salespeople don't know what to say when
> they first get through on the phone. Using a hook
> ensures there is no awkward silence which might
> enable the prospect to seize control of the
> conversation.*

Some examples are:

◆ 'I'm contacting all the top financial directors in
the area.'

◆ 'I see you're building a new warehouse in
Birmingham.'

◆ 'I read about the large order from Germany
your company's just won.'

- ◆ 'Mr Jim Perkins of XYZ Limited suggested I call you.'

- ◆ 'My sales director especially asked me to get in touch with you.'

The opening hot button statement that follows is a general 'what's in it for them' type. There are probably many advantages of your product or service which will apply to different people. Your best chance of making a successful call is when you make a statement that applies directly to the person you are talking to. You have to ask yourself the question, 'If I were in their position, what would interest me most about my product or service?' For example, the proprietor of a business or the managing director and financial director of a company are mainly interested in profit. Other employees look to making their jobs easier or getting recognition from their superiors for achievement. So before you make the call, you must sort out which statement is likely to apply to each buyer.

Here's an example: 'Mr Johnson, we've been able to assist a number of companies in a similar line to you to save up to 15% on their production costs. Now at this stage I have no idea whether we could do something similar for you. So what I would like to do is discuss one or two points. How does that sound to you?'

While probing is a series of open-ended questions, the final question must be a closed question to which the answer is 'yes', to confirm you're hitting the right spot – the hot button.

Salesperson	'So what you're saying is that service is important to you. Is that correct?'
Prospect	'Yes, absolutely.'
	(*Now ready for the pre-close stage*)
Salesperson	'If you were convinced that there was a company who could give you each of these things at a competitive price, you would certainly consider using them, wouldn't you?'
Prospect	'Yes, I would.'
	(*Now moving into the matching phase*)

| Salesperson | 'Fine, let me explain . . . /let us imagine . . . /let me tell you about . . .' |

You are now ready to match what you are offering to what the prospect wants – making contact with that hot button. Remember features which give the prospect benefits and include them in your telesales presentation, explaining what they mean to the customer's business and why they are of value:

◆ What the product or service is.

◆ What is new or different about the product or service.

◆ What the details are.

◆ The overall result of using the product or service.

Now confirm needs and match to benefits.

Selling benefits

Once you've established the needs of the prospective customer, you have your chance to exercise your selling skills and powers of persuasion. With the help of facts and figures about your company, you have got to show what you can do for them. You have to persuade the prospective customer that, based on their needs and requirements, it makes good sense to let your firm supply them. Don't go overboard at this stage about how marvellous your organisation is. Confine the facts and benefits to those which will obviously help the prospect with their wants and needs.

To convince the prospect still further that they will be making the right decision in giving you the business, it's worth confirming the points that you've established from the conversation by careful listening. Your approach could run along these lines:

> 'From what you've told me, you require and depend on regular deliveries of a wide range of items.'

The prospect might not have said this in actual words, but this is the gist of what was said in answer to your carefully phrased questions.

> *You and the prospect are now on common ground with a joint objective to work towards.*

This is why it pays to listen carefully. Even a throwaway comment from a prospective customer can be of value.

Once you have told the prospect about the benefits of buying from your firm, the next vital step is to get their reaction to the points you outlined. An attempt on your part to close the sale will usually do the trick. It is only then that you will find out what the customer really feels about all or some of the points you have made. Every sales call should come to a definite conclusion, not left hanging. On all calls it is essential a formal sales proposition is made by closing the sale.

Not all telesales calls end successfully. It could be that you might not get an order the first or even second time round. But by attempting to close the sale, you will have got the customer's reaction, which gives you something to go on in future.

Overcoming objections

There are two kinds of objection:

◆ frivolous

◆ serious, which are of three types

    1 technical or specific
    2 prejudicial
    3 undefined.

Purely frivolous objections can be by-passed or ignored altogether. Where objections are both frivolous and serious, deal with them this way, step by step:

◆ Classify them – frivolous, serious or both?

◆ Relax and keep your cool.

◆ Accept or agree.

◆ Question.

◆ Find an opening.

◆ Use the selling sequence.

◆ Cite a third party (as an example), benefits, investment, then close.

Questions are important because they:

◆ avoid argument

◆ enable you to determine the true objection

◆ enable you to make sure you fully understand

◆ enable you to find any hidden objection

◆ enable you to dispel the objection.

If an objection is raised that is going to interrupt or seriously affect your presentation, you must treat it as a serious objection and deal with it at once. Any objection can retard the progress of your sales interview. Most objections are the result of the prospective buyer's state of mind. Most are voiced, but sometimes hesitation at the other end of the line signifies an unspoken objection. In telephone selling you do not have the advantage of seeing facial expressions or other body language to tell you that your prospect is not in agreement with something.

Objections can arise in the prospect's mind for one or several of the following:

◆ Fear of change.

◆ A good reason for not buying or specifying at the present time.

◆ The prospect has not been given enough information.

◆ The prospect needs more justification to buy.

◆ Caused by poor selling because:
  (a) you present the case for your product or service badly

  (b) you are not communicating properly

  (c) you are exaggerating or misrepresenting the facts

  (d) you blind the prospect with science

  (e) you are raising negative ideas in the prospect's mind

  (f) you express the wrong application or benefits.

◆ The prospect has no confidence in you.

◆ Or even that the buyer is trying to unsettle you.

If your state of mind is one of uncertainty, the lack of confidence will show through in your voice and

prompt objections from the prospective buyer.
Reasons for this could be:

◆ You are apprehensive about possible objections.

◆ You do not know the benefits of your product
or service.

◆ You lack confidence in your product or service
itself.

◆ You are being negative and half-hearted.

◆ You have not found the requirements of the
prospect.

◆ You are unsettled by the conditions under
which you are operating.

◆ Through nervousness you talk continuously
without asking or listening.

◆ You are apprehensive about the prospect's
status.

Be upbeat about objections. An objection should
be welcomed not feared.

Anticipate normal standard objections which arise through competitors' propaganda or hearsay. These can often be pre-handled before they are raised and turned into selling benefits, to make the sale quicker.

Remember an objection often positively helps you by:

♦ showing how interested the prospective buyer is

♦ revealing the benefits in which the buyer is principally interested

♦ showing whether competition is present, and how strong it is

♦ showing buying signals.

Handle an objection immediately when:

♦ it is in the right place during the sales interview

♦ you cannot go on until the objection is handled

♦ the objection shows an area of real interest to the prospect

◆ your answer gives you an opportunity to close.

Defer handling an objection:

◆ to prevent you losing your train of thought

◆ in order to keep the initiative and control of
the call

◆ when you need time to think

◆ when you need to get an answer from someone
else

◆ when you can answer more positively later on.

When a prospect tells you the price is too high,
this could mean any of the following:

◆ 'More expensive than I thought.'

◆ 'More than I can authorise.'

◆ 'Outside my budget.'

◆ 'We have no money.'

◆ 'I'm not convinced of the value.'

◆ 'Somebody else is cheaper.'

◆ 'I want a discount.'

You must find out which is the real reason behind the objection in order to handle it, and this is where 'ask back' questions come into play:

◆ 'In relation to what?'

◆ 'What exactly to you mean by that?'

◆ 'I'm sure you have a very good reason for saying that – do you mind if I ask you what it is?

> *In certain cases, in trying to re-explain it to you, the prospect will have answered the objection themselves.*

Once you have been given a figure on which the prospect has based their price objection, explain to them the real worth and value of your product or service. Reduce in their eyes the price difference to the smallest possible amount. 'I can buy cheaper elsewhere' should be countered with, 'I'm sure you can, but let me ask you, how much cheaper?' Show that any difference is more than compensated for by extra matching value.

Sometimes it pays to agree with a prospect's viewpoint, because it softens objections in their mind and avoids confrontation. Useful phrases are 'I can understand that', 'I can appreciate that', 'That's a very good point, I'm glad you brought it up', 'I used to think the same myself', 'That's exactly the initial reaction of many of our best customers', 'Perhaps I didn't explain that point fully'.

When a competitor is mentioned, your approach should be as follows:

Prospect   'You're more expensive than . . .'

You   'That's correct, but isn't it true that all companies have a choice to make. They can either provide a service which does as much as possible for their customers *or* give a service just sufficient for them to get by with. Isn't that the choice every company has to make?'

Prospect   'Yes.'

You   'What would you like us to do, provide a good service or one just enough for your company to get by with?'

Then you remind the prospect of matching benefits and remember to add that extra special value your company has to offer.

Closing the sale

All telesales calls to prospective buyers should have a close, where you achieve a firm commitment regarding action to be taken immediately or at a mutually agreed date later on. Ideally, of course, we all intend to close by securing an order, but a close can be any action decision which is agreed between the prospective buyer and you as the salesperson.

The object of making our telephone sales pitch is to find out what the prospect wants and then match to it. Once we've achieved this, we ask for the order. But if we ask for the order before we've completed the matching, we're likely to face objections. The right time to ask a closing question is when the matching is complete. This is a crucial stage, so first test you've got the matching right by asking a test close question. This is a question the answer to which confirms that the prospect is sold on your product or service, or at least is well on the way to being sold. Some examples of test close questions are:

◆ 'How do you feel about that?'

◆ 'Are you happy with everything?'

◆ 'How does that strike you?'

◆ 'Do you have a date in mind?'

◆ 'Do you have any other questions?'

Assuming the prospect is completely happy, you can move directly into the closing question. If not, trial closes can be used to determine how far you have managed to get the prospect's interest towards the final close. Trial closes can be useful for uncovering objections in the prospect's mind as well as revealing where their chief interest lies. Almost any question assuming the prospect is going to buy can be used as a trial close. For example:

◆ 'Which is most convenient – delivery by road or rail?'

◆ 'Would you prefer a plain or decorative finish?'

Often the prospective buyer will send out signals showing they have come to a decision to buy by asking you questions that exhibit interest in such details as, for example, after-sales service or delivery dates. When, following trial closes and buying signals from the customer, you judge the time is right for the final close, use any of the following methods singly or in combination:

◆ The 'ask for it' close. This is the best and most logical close, provided you have done a good job of selling to the point where the prospect is very close to giving you an order.

> *This is the least used because many salespeople fear the answer will be 'no'. But a reason is given for most refusals, which is in effect an objection to be overcome. A 'no' need not mark the end of your telesales call.*

◆ 'Summary of benefits' close. This enables you to remind the prospect of the reasons for buying your product or service.

◆ 'Continued affirmation' close. Similar to the previous close, but one in which you get the prospect to say 'yes' to each benefit presented to them logically step by step.

- 'Logical' close. Where a prospective buyer specifies criteria which must be satisfied, the salesperson summarises the ways in which the product or service takes care of these points. This can be a very effective way of leading up to a direct request for an order.

- 'Alternative' close is where you give the prospect two alternatives, such as 'Would you prefer . . . or . . .?', both being acceptable to your own firm.

- 'Assumptive' close. You assume the prospect has bought your product or service and ask them a question of a minor nature, such as:

  (a) 'Where would you like it sent?'

  (b) 'Do we send the invoice to you directly?'

  (c) 'Could I just confirm your name and address for delivery?'

  (d) 'What publicity literature or point of sale material would you like?'

- 'Special inducement' close, consisting of premium or other temporary advantages which will be lost if the prospect does not order right away, can be used to overcome delaying tactics.

The follow-up call

When making a follow-up call, don't expect the customer to instantly remember you and what you discussed. Begin by introducing yourself again to the customer before picking up the threads of your previous conversation.

> *Instead of 'It's me again', introduce yourself in full with your firm's name.*

Start off with some more open-ended questions, because by asking these to gain more facts you're also helping to jog the customer's memory about who you are and your line of business. Those extra details you gain may also help you put a better proposition to the customer. Having talked for a while, go through the benefits and close the sale.

Incidentally, if you do send out literature to a customer for their interest or to back up your previous phone call, ensure you address it by name to the person for whom it is intended. Otherwise it could be lost in the vast pile of literature received daily in every office which ends up in the wastepaper bin. Write a message on the accompanying compliment slip clearly indicating the relevant points you want to get over to the customer.

In summary...

◆ **Probe to find out what the customer wants (the hot button).**

◆ **Match the benefits of your product or service to the hot button.**

◆ **Let objections work to your advantage.**

◆ **Master all forms of the trial close.**

◆ **Choose the right moment for the vital final close.**

Always remember – Sell! Sell! Sell!